S0-AEB-695

ONE-MINUTE PRAYERS® for Wives

HOPE LYDA

HARVEST HOUSE PUBLISHERS
EUGENE, OREGON

Cover by Bryce Williamson

To Marc, a man of remarkable grace and strength.

ONE-MINUTE PRAYERS® FOR WIVES

Published by Harvest House Publishers
Eugene, Oregon 97402
www.harvesthousepublishers.com

ISBN 978-0-7369-6995-6 (pbk.)
ISBN 978-0-7369-6996-3 (eBook)

Printed in the China

17 18 19 20 21 22 23 24 25 / RDS-GL / 10 9 8 7 6 5 4 3 2 1

Contents

GRATITUDE

Glad for Beginnings

*The fear of the LORD is the beginning of wisdom;
all who follow his precepts have good
understanding. To him belongs eternal praise.*

PSALM 111:10

What would I do without beginnings, God? When my vision gets cloudy and I cannot clearly see the gifts of the present day or the possibilities for the future, I know that I need to start my movement along the path You have prepared for me. It's the way of wisdom and understanding. It offers assurances of next steps and a forward direction even when I can't figure out what is unfolding.

When my husband and I find ourselves at crossroads or dead ends, we know it's because we have been wandering in our own understanding. Each time is an opportunity to shed our flawed human perspective and look ahead with Your eyes. And each new beginning with You is bright with hope.

The Way of Water

Forget the former things; do not dwell on the past. See, I am doing a new thing! Now it springs up; do you not perceive it?

Isaiah 43:18

I have been changed by Your living water, God. It refreshes me in my desert-dry days when I'm thirsty for a life of value. It lifts me up in waves of compassion when I experience storms of grief. You've let me surf its crests so You could carry me away from the past and toward new shores. When I've forgotten which way to go as a woman, as a wife, You call me to follow the waterways that lead me back to the source of Your love.

Lord, You gently baptize me in this water. I am made clean and new. My cupped hands that once held worries are filling with the drops of Your living water from heaven. Without fear, I sip from the sustenance You offer because I know my outreached hands will be filled again tomorrow.

Blessing in the Waiting

Lord, I wait for you; you will answer, Lord my God.

Psalm 38:15

God, You are showing me the gift of these waiting seasons when I'm actively listening, praying, calling out to You, and being still before You. This used to be my crazy place. My mind and heart would make up doubts until I was convinced that You would never respond. Now, I hold on to the truth that You *will* answer and You *are* with me during these seasons. This eases my spirit and shushes my internal chatter. I prepare space in my life to be with You, and I prepare a place within me to receive Your answer and presence with gratitude.

I pray that my new perspective of patience pleases You, Lord. Honoring You is another way these formerly daunting times are transformed into blessings.

Growing My Gratitude

Keep your roots deep in him,
build your lives on him,
and become stronger in your faith,
as you were taught.
And be filled with thanksgiving.

COLOSSIANS 2:7 GNT

Lord, recently when I spoke words of thanksgiving, there were echoes of frustration in my heart that rang more true than the words of grace I said aloud. I don't want my circumstances to undermine my thankfulness. When my faith is rooted deep in Your promises, there won't be a disconnect between what I profess and what I later confess to You in the stillness of my prayer time.

I want to live and love from an undivided heart. When my husband and I face trials and celebrate milestones, may the thanksgiving pour from me with sincerity. There will be winds of change that cause us to bend, but with our lives rooted in Your strength, we will not break.

Joy

The Joy of the Harvest

The Lord your God will bless
you in all your harvest
and in all the work of your hands,
and your joy will be complete.

Deuteronomy 16:15

I don't till the earth, but I do plant seeds. I don't gather grain in the fields, but I do have a life that bears a harvest. You bless me, Lord, with work to do and seasons of growth. I tend to my marriage and watch it bloom with love. I make prayer a priority, and faith takes root. Each day's toil nourishes my family and they flourish as a result of that investment of intention. With joy I anticipate the fruit of Your labor, not mine. I believe that You have planted seeds within me that You're still tending to. I know that I'll continue to grow and reach new heights in the warmth of Your sun. I am so grateful for the harvest of Your love in my life.

Share in the Glorious Feast

Nehemiah said, "Go and enjoy choice food and sweet drinks, and send some to those who have nothing prepared. This day is holy to our Lord. Do not grieve, for the joy of the Lord *is your strength."*

Nehemiah 8:10

Life is a fabulous feast! Truly. I'm so thankful for the buffet of goodness that lays before me. You have given to me the sweetness of love with my husband, the taste of kinship with my friends, and the chance to break bread with a community of believers. How can I ever speak of hunger again? In the times when I want for something, whether it is comfort or change or answers from You, the joy that comes from You is the nourishment I need to strengthen me and fill any void that makes itself known. From all that I've been given, lead me to share with others. Give me eyes to see when another is hungry for a bit of what I have to offer. And give me a heart to share Your immeasurable joy, Lord.

Surprised by Your Goodness

You make me glad by your deeds, Lord;
I sing for joy at what your hands have done.

Psalm 92:4

Lord, You have surprised me again with signs of Your care. When I was feeling alone You brought people to inquire about me. And when I was discouraged over a conversation with my husband, You gave us a point of connection during the day that turned us both toward laughter. I believe it is easier to dwell on what causes agitation than on what causes gladness. But I'm going to aim my gaze higher than the trouble that might trip up my feet. Instead, I will look up to see the good things that fall from above. Now I will understand how many are being scattered over my life because I will notice them, and my open heart will receive them with happiness and gratitude.

Encouraging Words

A person finds joy in giving an apt reply—
and how good is a timely word!

PROVERBS 15:23

God, give me the heart of an encourager so that I can be quick to offer my husband words of cheer, support, insight, and thoughtfulness. I can spend a lot of thought considering how to be a good friend to my girlfriends but I assume my support for my husband will just happen naturally. He knows I love him, right? Then I recall how my mood, day, and disposition are transformed when my husband speaks joy and reassurance into my life. I long to be a wife who sees my husband's heart and reflects back to him his goodness and the potential You see in him. What does his spirit need today? Prompt me toward the right word at the right time so he feels buoyed by being known and loved fully.

Grace

A Positive Influence

When [Barnabas] arrived and saw what the grace of God had done, he was glad and encouraged them all to remain true to the Lord with all their hearts.

Acts 11:23

Simple graciousness is lost in the frenzy that buzzes around me and, I must admit, within me some days. And because of this, Your grace has even greater positive influence. People are stunned when they receive a touch of it from someone else. Lord, I want to be a woman who extends Your grace to everyone and who never worries about whether they offer it back to me. It's okay if others are frugal with their version. That should motivate me to shower those people with more of Your mercy and love. Nobody is immune to the influence of Your sweet grace for very long. It makes us feel held and safe. And in these times of hyperconnection that results in frequent isolation, feeling held and safe changes us inside out.

In Perfect Balance

Where sin increased, grace increased all the more.

Romans 5:20

Today I think about how my interaction with my husband has been. Lord, my marital kindness report card often humbles me. My good intentions are pushed aside by self-centered priorities and my desire to be right or in control. As discouraged as I am, I rest in Your grace, which rises to meet my sin. You balance me, and You encourage me to seek Your grace and the transformation that is possible in that grace.

I face another series of days to be loving, attentive, and forgiving. You bless me with a chance to be a vessel of Your love for my husband. May I let go of self-serving actions and desires so that there is more and more room in my heart for Your grace.

I Am What I Am

By the grace of God I am what I am, and his grace to me was not without effect.
No, I worked harder than all of them—yet not I, but the grace of God that was with me.

1 Corinthians 15:10

"I am what I am" was character Popeye's saying and I'm thinking it might be a good one for me to adopt. There was a time when I would've said that phrase to "prove" I can't change, that I am what I am and the other person just has to live with it. That isn't how I take that sentiment now. In fact, it is the opposite. The verse in Corinthians reminds me that I am only this far along in life and in love because of Your good grace, Lord. I'm thankful that I can keep changing into Your likeness. I strive for certain accomplishments, Lord, but any blessing that has come into my home, marriage, and personal life is straight from Your generous hand. I am what I am but only, dear Lord, because You are what You are.

At All Times

And God is able to make all grace abound to you, so that in all things at all times, having all that you need, you will abound in every good work.

2 Corinthians 9:8

How many steps forward have my husband and I put off because we were waiting for everything to line up just right? How often have we said, "If only we had this, then for sure we could move ahead on that"? God, don't You tire of us holding back and holding up the good works You want us to see through to fruition?

Help us believe that at all times there's nothing we need to achieve, gather, or acquire before we follow Your will and abound in every good work You set in motion for us. God, let us be fully aware that the great things and the small things that express Your love are all possible in Your strength and grace. Find us faithful, dear Lord.

Wholeness

Seeing God in My Marriage

No one has ever seen God;
but if we love one another,
God lives in us and his love is
made complete in us.

1 John 4:12

There are times when I can list off the things my husband is doing wrong. What a terrible thing to admit, Lord. I am dropping that mental list and only keeping track of the ways that I see You in him. How is Your grace evident in his forgiveness? How is Your strength and help made clear in his efforts to lead us? How has his own transformation in even small ways shown to me the power of Your salvation? I realize now that this positive, faithful list can go on and on. I will be a better friend and partner and lover when I find the wholeness of Your love within my marriage. Help me to watch for You and Your love in my husband and in this relationship from this day forward.

Squinting and Scared

I will lead the blind by ways they have not known,
along unfamiliar paths I will guide them;
I will turn the darkness into light before
them and make the rough places smooth.

Isaiah 42:16

You didn't give me the ability to see and know the future for good reason. In the unknowing, I am to lean upon Your sure provision and nothing else. In this place of surrender and vulnerability, You call me back to Your presence for all things...this is always the starting place and ending place for peace. In the unknowing we are to lean into You and lean upon You with certainty and joy, not fear.

I want to have the security and wholeness of this peace, Lord. Instead of squinting in the dark and imagining the worst up ahead, I will trust You to shed light on the path and to smooth the way so my progress brings You praise and glory.

In Front of Everyone

Then the woman, seeing that she could not go unnoticed, came trembling and fell at his feet. In the presence of all the people, she told why she had touched him and how she had been instantly healed. Then he said to her, "Daughter, your faith has healed you. Go in peace."

LUKE 8:47-48

I am strong in my faith, Lord, but sometimes I'm a bit shy about sharing Your wonders in my life. This makes me feel false. Or as though I'm only giving the people around me *half* the story of my journey, my struggles, and the sweet times of healing.

Like the woman who reached with faith to touch Your garment, I want to stand in the presence of all the people I love, know, or encounter and speak of my Lord and my wholeness with great vulnerability. I might be trembling when I do it, but the peace will come and I will carry it with me after as I keep walking, reaching, and sharing with faith. You make my story whole, Lord. Thank You.

In Love and in Like

Therefore, if you have any encouragement from being united with Christ, if any comfort from his love, if any common sharing in the Spirit, if any tenderness and compassion, then make my joy complete by being like-minded, having the same love, being one in spirit and of one mind.

PHILIPPIANS 2:1-2

We had one of those arguments, God. Now that the tears and the tension have cleared, I come to You with my open hands and heart. You comfort me in the awkward silence, and You prompt me to go to my husband with the same open hands and heart. And when I do, I feel the tenderness of Your compassion and his.

Our love for You is our common ground. Even if we are in the middle of a disagreement, we can stand in our mutual faith with joy. And when we do, I vividly remember why I first fell in like with my husband before I fell in love with him—because he is made in *Your* likeness. I am blessed.

Seeking Wisdom

Beyond All Else

Can you discover the limits and bounds of the greatness and power of God? The sky is no limit for God, but it lies beyond your reach... God's greatness is broader than the earth, wider than the sea.

JOB 11:7-9 GNT

Praise should be my daily offering. Often my wants and cries for help rise to the top of my prayers, and I leave little time for singing Your praises. Well, today will be different. Your goodness is beyond any kindness I have ever received. Your grace is beyond any human forgiveness I've ever been extended. Your power is beyond any I have ever witnessed in man-made attempts to show strength or smarts. And Your greatness surpasses even the wonders of Your creation! It hits me afresh that I am in daily partnership with the God who is beyond all else and loves *me* beyond all measure. In Your hand, I feel small and significant at the same time. Oh, Lord, I praise You with all that I am.

Thirsty Marriage

You, God, are my God, earnestly I seek you;
I thirst for you, my whole body longs for you,
in a dry and parched land where there is no water.

Psalm 63:1

God, I seek Your sustenance for my marriage. Let Your love and wisdom rain down on us. I don't want to let a hurting time turn into a dry season. Refuel our connection so that we don't let small talk become our only conversation. Restore our first instincts to be tender with one another's heart and protective of our love.

I long to feel Your hand on our marriage when we seem extra fragile. Refill us with Your living water so we become alive again and eager to put in the work, effort, care, and commitment to build on the foundation of love we have and are grateful for. Guide us to discover the deeper hope You have planted in our relationship. It will not wither, but will flourish in Your care. Refresh us, Lord.

Hidden Treasure

Beg for knowledge; plead for insight.
Look for it as hard as you would for silver
or some hidden treasure. If you do, you will
know what it means to fear the Lord
and you will succeed in learning about God.

Proverbs 2:3-5 gnt

God, my husband and I desperately need Your wisdom for a current decision. We both switch from opinionated to unsure. I think we're afraid of speaking too strongly in favor of one direction and then having it be a misstep. Here's the truth...we don't know which way to go. I seek Your wisdom and leading, God. Grant us patience and discernment so that we don't rush toward an answer just to have an answer. Then grant us peace as we step forward knowing that no matter which direction we go, our priority is to seek Your presence and the hidden treasure of Your wisdom with each step. We don't have to know outcomes to know the purpose in trusting You.

Embracing Wisdom

Do not abandon wisdom, and she will protect you; love her, and she will keep you safe. Getting wisdom is the most important thing you can do. Whatever else you get, get insight. Love wisdom, and she will make you great. Embrace her, and she will bring you honor. She will be your crowning glory.

PROVERBS 4:6-9 GNT

A friend asked me what objects I would grab first if our house caught on fire. I thought about a few keepsakes that have sentimental value. But otherwise, there are not many things I would face the fire for. I like this realization that what I want to hold and protect and keep safe is not a purchased treasure, but is Your truth, hope, and love. I don't need things for assurance or peace. My security in life and in my marriage truly comes from Your presence. I'm thankful that I finally *get* this. Let me embrace and not let go of Your wisdom. My heart is content with all that You provide. May this perspective and way of being honor You, Lord.

Healing

You Hear Me

LORD my God, I called to you for help and you healed me.

PSALM 30:2

When I have a day that begins with tears, my heart's desire is to be in Your presence without distractions. I need this down time to be lifted up by Your love, Lord. You know my scars, the wounds that are still healing, and the places that I have yet to fully offer up to Your light and healing. You are so patient with me. If I had wandered the earth when You did, Jesus, I would've walked along the edges of Your crowd, always curious but also anxious about bringing all of me to You as a living sacrifice. Today, I quicken my step to be right beside You. And when You look at me, I will nod to You. This is the day I want You to know and heal all of me, Jesus.

Love Rising

Rise up and help us; redeem us
because of your unfailing love.

Psalm 44:26

Redeem this marriage, God. Look it over from every angle. What aspects are to be elevated? Removed? Transformed? My husband and I offer our relationship to You for Your purposes. May You rise up in our lives. May others see Your strength in our struggles. Your unfailing love is the only thing that can save our fallible, human love. We trust Your healing even in times when we harbor doubts about ourselves or the other. Thank You for allowing us to see our own flaws more clearly so that we look to Your perfection for our answers. There's nothing that we have created that can serve as our foundation. Only You and Your healing mercy provide that place for us to stand together with hope and the great peace of Your promises.

Shiny and New

Restore us, O God; make your face shine upon us, that we may be saved.

Psalm 80:19

I've always loved the moon. It reminds me of Your presence when the sky turns dark and my thoughts follow. But today I give my imagination over to thoughts of You as the sun. Your brilliance shining above me to provide warmth for my skin, my heart, my cells. You shed light on circumstances so my husband and I can see truth and the way to go. When I am tired and find the daily routine more draining than encouraging, You give me energy and hope. Lord, restore me as a living offering that pleases You. I don't want to be lackluster and half-hearted about this life of mine. You bless me richly. Give me the desire to turn my face and spirit to You so I can be saved by Your light, Lord. Make me shiny and new for You.

I Heard You

Gracious words are a honeycomb, sweet to the soul and healing to the bones.

Proverbs 16:24

Ah, thank You for the gentle and gracious words, Lord. You spoke them to my hurting heart through my husband and then again through a friend. They didn't know about the ache that I was tending to in my spirit, but You did. You see every part of me, and You know when I am inclined to retreat rather than to seek the care I need. Thank You for Your sweetness. I had no doubt that the provision of soothing words of hope and peace were from Your heart. Not only did these dear exchanges make me fall in love with You all over again, they made me feel even more connected to my husband and present to my friend. Such gifts come along with Your care, Lord. I will savor today's healing.

Commitment

The Cause of Love

Commit your way to the Lord;
trust in him and he will do this:
He will make your righteous reward shine like the dawn, your vindication like the noonday sun.

Psalm 37:5-6

As I find peace in this love You have given to me, I want to know how to truly be committed to love. I lean against Your Word and Your promises so that I understand what it means to be faithful and true to another. You are my example of love and kindness. I pray to be more like You each day.

I commit this marriage to You, Lord. My life. His life. And this shared experience that takes on a life of its own. These are my offerings to You. May they become my cause, and may You shine Your love upon it and give it life, energy, and purpose.

Lifting Up Another

Now I commit you to God and to the word of his grace, which can build you up and give you an inheritance among all those who are sanctified.

Acts 20:32

Today I lift up my husband in prayer. I want his life to be in Your hands, Lord. Sometimes I try to be the one to bring him peace and comfort. You call me to try...to have compassion and to offer constant support. But I know that when it comes to matters of his heart and life and purpose...You are the one who needs to build him up and direct him.

Help me to stay out of the way when space is needed. Guide me to step up to the promises I made to this person when it is my turn. Lead me along the way of unwavering commitment as I pray daily for this person who knows and loves me.

Honesty

Whoever of you loves life and
desires to see many good days,
keep your tongue from evil and
your lips from telling lies.

Psalm 34:12-13

I love this life. When I awaken to a new day and realize all that You have for me to do, to say, to accomplish, to consider, to pray about...I feel very blessed. Give me a spirit of honesty and sincerity as I live this life. May my thoughts turn to my good fortune and to my love for You when I am tempted to speak against another or tear down goodness in any way.

My words can harm my marriage and my husband and my own sense of worth. Breathe new words into my vocabulary that support this commitment I have made.

Faithfulness

Keep your lives free from the love of money
and be content with what you have,
because God has said, "Never will I
leave you; never will I forsake you."

HEBREWS 13:5

Reveal to me my unfaithful tendencies, God. Even if I am faithful physically, I know there are different ways that I betray my marriage love. My priorities get off-kilter, and pretty soon I am putting my financial security or wants ahead of my marriage's well-being.

Lord, release me from the self-imposed pressure of perfection and idealism. Bring me back to the real needs that exist in my life. When I stray and seek to satisfy my lust for a different life, remind me of what I would be sacrificing. I pray to always honor my husband and the life we share by never sacrificing the wrong things in my pursuit of personal gain.

PATIENCE

The Bridge to Compassion

A person's wisdom yields patience; it is to one's glory to overlook an offense.

PROVERBS 19:11

I am just learning how to hold my tongue and my patience. I used to have to tap my foot and roll my eyes as I waited out my anger or judgment. But You have given me renewed strength. I feel You controlling my emotions, and this releases me from the burden. Time and mistakes and missteps have given me wisdom to deal with the mistakes of others.

Calm my heart and my mind when they are raging toward accusation and frustration. Allow me a bridge of compassion so that I can step above and over the hurdle before me. On the other side I will find the beauty of forgiveness and mercy. I will experience the freedom of overlooking the flaws and human ways of another.

Eating of the Fruit

But the fruit of the Spirit is love, joy, peace, forbearance, kindness, goodness, faithfulness, gentleness and self-control.

Galatians 5:22-23

Oh, how I am like Eve when I shouldn't be! I want to eat of the fruit when You ask me not to. Each bite brings with it pride, selfishness, greed, and fear. But the fruit of the Spirit...the fruit I should be consuming with great gusto...is often left off my plate. Is it because the lessons are difficult to learn? Do I like where I am at emotionally?

Lord, serve up the fruit of the Spirit. Let my soul taste the wonders of Christlike behavior. I long to be a person who loves, who is joyful, who is patient, kind, good, faithful, gentle, and self-controlled. I pray to feast on these fruits daily so that they become my source of nourishment.

I Am Such an Example

But for that very reason I was shown mercy
so that in me, the worst of sinners,
Christ Jesus might display his immense
patience as an example for those who would
believe in him and receive eternal life.

1 Timothy 1:16

Though I am not always proud of how much mercy I require, I do believe my life has been an example to others. The way of life and marriage and family is not so easy. I do stumble. I do need mercy in bulk. But those who really know me, including my husband, also witness Your incredible patience with me.

I don't mind being the walking, talking example of Your grace, Lord. If I cannot accept the humility of this role, I had better forget becoming a person of deeper faith. Because each time I fail and You prevail I am leading others in the direction of Your forgiveness and eternal life.

Show Me the Way

We do not want you to become lazy,
but to imitate those who through faith and
patience inherit what has been promised.

HEBREWS 6:12

Lately I have not been following any good examples of patience. I seem to be following the beat of a very fast rhythm created by the culture around me. I can go for days being patient and understanding, and then the next thing I know, I am mad at how slowly the earth is moving beneath me. Nothing is happening as it should. I feel behind and lost and off course.

Grant me the serenity of Your pace for my life, Lord. Give me examples in the people I meet and speak to. When I grow impatient with a person, show me how to love him or her in that moment. When I grow impatient with the progress of my life, show me my inheritance in You so that my spirit will rest in the rhythms of Your way.

Dependence

Where I Stand

My salvation and my honor depend on God; he is my mighty rock, my refuge.

Psalm 62:7

My identity takes shape through my marriage, my work, my effort spent in the world. What I forget, however, is that my identity should be grounded in You. Forgive me for always looking to the material aspects of my life or to my obvious roles as my source of honor, strength, and worth. I should be looking at my source and foundation...and that is You.

Lead me back to stand on the rock of my salvation and faith. All that is of value and worth comes from Your heart and hand. May I not depend on anything else.

Submission

Wives, submit yourselves to your husbands, as is fitting in the Lord.

Colossians 3:18

You won't be surprised by this because You know me, but I struggle with submitting to my husband. Or to anyone/anything in authority. Even when I come to pray to You and step into Your presence I know my heart is not as humble as it should be. God, I ask to have a heart that gives itself willingly to love, to faith, and to my marriage.

When my pride and self-assurance block my ability to be dependent in a healthy way, I lose my opportunity to understand faith and grace. Guide me toward a balanced sense of submission. Humble my heart so that I honor my husband and You and my life with a new freedom.

I Don't Get It

Trust in the LORD *with all your heart and*
lean not on your own understanding;
in all your ways submit to him, and
he will make your paths straight.

PROVERBS 3:5-6

I don't get life. And if I am honest with myself...I never will. I don't think You call me to totally understand everything that happens to me, to my family, or to my friends. Where my faith can lead me, however, is to Your understanding of trials, joy, miracles, and suffering. I might not see the big picture, but I can depend on Your perspective to be the truth.

All I do know is that I have a love for You that is strong. I do believe in Your ways and look forward to discovering the path You have for me. Even if each turn of a corner brings questions, I can rest in Your knowing and understanding.

A Lesson Revisited

If anyone acknowledges that
Jesus is the Son of God, God lives
in them and they in God.
And so we know and rely on
the love God has for us.

1 JOHN 4:15-16

I spent much of my youth struggling to be self-reliant. Even as I became a person of faith, I found myself turning back to the security of my capabilities and successes. Yet I fail. I step where I should jump. I sleep when I should be awake. I rush when I should be lingering. When will I learn the lesson of loving You?

Restore in me that hunger to trust You and to rely on Your love. When I was a child, I sought the shelter of my father and mother's love. Guide me back to the comfort of Your sheltering mercy.

Partnership

Connected by the Spirit

Since we live by the Spirit,
let us keep in step with the Spirit.
Let us not become conceited,
provoking and envying each other.

Galatians 5:25-26

I have come to realize that marriage is a supernatural entity. When I turn to my own abilities and strength, I do not have what it takes to serve my marriage. But when I partner with the Spirit, I am able to partner with another person and move that relationship forward.

Lord, help me to stay focused on this connection with the Spirit. May I not act out in envy, judgment, or arrogance toward my husband when I become disconnected from You. I pray to stay tethered to You so that I can remain a faithful, loving, kind partner all my days.

Help Wanted

Submit to one another out of reverence for Christ.

Ephesians 5:21

God, lead me to a mentor. I seek Your wisdom and Your Word, but I also need people in my life with whom I can feel safe and secure and nurtured. Help me recognize those people in my life now. Show me how to submit to a new or even an established relationship so that I might learn and glean from it.

I see Your hand in my life, Lord. And I know You direct my steps. I trust You to show me how to partner with others as I continue along the path You have for me. Show me how to have a deeper connection with my husband, with a mentor, and with those who can teach me more about You.

Where Is the Love?

Finally, all of you, be like-minded, be sympathetic, love one another, be compassionate and humble.

1 Peter 3:8

Some days the love for my husband is hidden deep within me. So hidden in fact, that I struggle to access it in the middle of a moment. I'm tired. Worn out. Hurried. Scattered. And taking the time to find the love I have for him is not always on my priority list.

Help me feel Your love, Lord, and pass it on to my husband. When I am trying to remember all the reasons I love my life partner…remind me of Your goodness and compassion. Reveal to me the tenderness of an inspired love for another. Give me Your heart and perspective when mine are not the best examples of lovingkindness.

A Faith Held Together

So be on your guard, and do not be unfaithful.

Malachi 2:16

I need Your protection, God. Lately my life has been a bit too much about me and not enough about You or the relationships You place in my life. I have felt distant from my husband and have not sought to understand his heart and needs. Protect me from indifference. Direct me to renew my commitment to hold fast to my faith and to my marriage. Give me the nourishment I need to pass along to those I love. Grant me a spirit that is faithful and generous so that I can serve my beliefs and priorities.

Self

A New Attitude

Do not lie to each other, since you have taken off your old self with its practices and have put on the new self, which is being renewed in knowledge in the image of its Creator.

Colossians 3:9-11

Bring on the new attitude I need to be a better wife. I am thankful for the love You have given to me. I appreciate each day that I grow to better understand my husband and what a blessing he is. But sometimes I revert to my old ways. I become frustrated if life is not perfect. That is an attitude I thought I had given up long ago. It serves no end except disappointment.

Give me a heart for truth and knowledge. Let my measure of a good life be made in smiles, commitment, and faith. Let this new attitude be the way I approach every good thing that comes from You.

Every Bit of Me

For you created my inmost being;
you knit me together in my mother's womb.
I praise you because I am fearfully
and wonderfully made;
your works are wonderful,
I know that full well.

Psalm 139:13-14

Remind me who I am, Lord. When I lose myself in my everyday life and cannot recall the passions and gifts that are mine...I can always turn to You. You are my touchstone and my creator. Everything I do, say, and am is noticed by You. When I am scared of what the future might bring, may I never second guess who I am in You.

If my sense of self takes over my faith, remind me who created me in my mother's womb. Remove the doubt that can undermine the strength You instill in me. And let me love my life just as You love me, Your child.

A Heart for Him

Do nothing out of selfish ambition or vain conceit. Rather, in humility value others above yourselves, not looking to your own interests but each of you to the interests of others.

PHILIPPIANS 2:3-4

Once I step outside of my personal wants, needs, and ambitions, I have the opportunity to see the needs of my husband. When I can push aside my desire to be right, I can hear what he is sharing. This marriage is strengthened when I first turn to You and pray to know my husband better.

Open my eyes to what is right in front of me. Let the walls of pride and personal objectives tumble down. After the dust settles, Your light will show me the ways I can serve my husband.

Intentions for a Full Life

May he give you the desire of your heart
and make all your plans succeed.

Psalm 20:4

Lord, You know the desires of my heart. Some I have put aside because the timing is not right. Others I have sacrificed for good reasons...and I don't have regrets. But there are other dreams and desires deep within me that long to be rescued from the mundane. I pray that You hear these and understand that sometimes I might not ask in the best way. My intention is good...I want to live life fully and with passion.

I want success that comes from Your hand. It doesn't have to involve wealth, fame, or influence. I just want to fully realize the potential You have planted in me. I want to embrace the desires that unfold now and later in my life.

LIFE

Celebrating Together

They celebrate your abundant goodness and joyfully sing of your righteousness.

Psalm 145:7

Show me how to embrace life. Teach me and my husband how to truly celebrate the gift of our days. When we drag our feet, teach us to dance. When our hearts are heavy with worldly pressures, lift us above the world. Put a song in my heart that I want to…no… that I long to share with everyone.

God, when my husband and I serve one another, let us rejoice in the doing. May our efforts at praise and celebration bring You joy and our lives peace.

Embracing Life

Now choose life, so that you and your children may live and that you may love the LORD your God, listen to his voice, and hold fast to him.

DEUTERONOMY 30:19-20

The choice should be easy. Choosing life should be obvious to one who is living and who cares about things of faith. But I can look back on my recent days and see where I have chosen things that do not enrich or enliven life. I take power from people with my negativity. I distance my heart from You when I refuse to give myself over to Your grace.

Lord, I want to embrace life and everything that breathes air into the lungs of my existence. You are the source of all that lives. May I draw close to Your voice, Your face, and Your ways so that I can bring to my marriage a sense of purpose and meaning.

Only the Names Have Been Changed

But now, this is what the Lord says—he who created you, Jacob, he who formed you, Israel: "Do not fear, for I have redeemed you; I have summoned you by name; you are mine."

RUTH 1:20-21

Do I hear You when You call me by name? You speak life into my daily routine by shouting words of significance and beauty. But do I listen? Sometimes I do not respond when You call me Your child. My ears are closed because I think I am not worthy to be called Your own. But You are faithful, patient, and strong.

Let my ears be open to hearing my name. When You call me Your daughter...Your chosen child...bless me with a receptive heart. My life depends on knowing You. I must listen when You call me to live in truth.

Resting in the Sun

Life will be brighter than noonday,
and darkness will become like morning.
You will be secure, because there is hope; you
will look about you and take your rest in safety.

Job 11:17-18

Open the windows of my soul. Grant me a seat from which I can view the great light that You shine on my life. Tear down the curtains that keep out the warmth of Your countenance. Give me security to bring my marriage out into the day. The brightness will expose its flaws, its bumps, its broken places.

But in Your hands, old things are made new. Restoration is possible. When my husband and I give our lives over to the dawn of Your direction, You make us whole again.

Sharing

Telling the Story

I pray that your partnership with us in the faith may be effective in deepening your understanding of every good thing we share for the sake of Christ.

PHILEMON 1:6

When I share the story of how my husband and I got together, I always return to an understanding of Your goodness. How amazing that our paths crossed and our eyes met…and we grew to love each other. Every love story opens up a deeper sense of how You give us life and purpose.

I pray to be a willing storyteller. May I share with others how I met You and came to know Your love. Telling this love story might lead others to Your heart. It also inspires others to share their own tales of finding faith. And each time I hear of Your faithfulness in another's life, I fall in love once again.

Communion

Because we loved you so much,
we were delighted to share with you
not only the gospel of God but our lives as well.

1 THESSALONIANS 2:8

Lord, give me the spirit of communion each day of my life. When I come to Your table, I sense the unity I have with others who believe and share in the cup... and in the bread. This is the blood of Christ. This is the body of Christ. This is being part of Your family. When I share with others this moment at the table, I am inviting them to experience the gospel.

My heart for those in the body is strong, Lord. May I go beyond the invitation to the table and begin to invite them into my life. This comes with risks and lots of "what if" questions, but it is in sharing my life that it becomes meaningful and usable by You.

Thankfulness

I will sacrifice a thank offering to you
and call on the name of the Lord.

Psalm 116:17

What do You call me to sacrifice? As I look around at all the trappings I have allowed into my home and life, I realize there is much to give up. There are parts of my life that have value and significance in Your eyes, and these too might be things You call me to offer to You with thanksgiving.

When my words of gratitude become slightly rote and flat...return me to the act of sacrifice. It is in the tearing away and paring away that my dependence on You returns.

Something Borrowed

Give to the one who asks you,
and do not turn away
from the one who wants to borrow from you.

MATTHEW 5:42

Let me give freely to those who ask. Allow me to see those needs that are not mentioned so I can give even more. Remind me that my own family is asking for things that I can give...time, love, connection. Help me put aside my worries and give freely, never fretting that what I give will be the last of what I have.

When my husband does not know how to ask for the things that fill his heart, tug on my own heart so that I can be sensitive to his wants and needs. God, never let me hold tightly to my blessings. These are meant to be shared.

SUPPORT

Make Me a Builder

Therefore encourage one another and build each other up, just as in fact you are doing.

1 Thessalonians 5:11

Do I construct or deconstruct the life You have blessed me with? I know what I want to be...a builder, a creator, a nurturer. But I get ahead of myself...and in my quest to build the perfect life, I tear down the imperfections or failings of others and even myself. A woman cannot build a life on a crumbling foundation. I require Your strength to mend the spirits of those around me with encouragement and comfort.

Make me a builder, Lord. Give me the tools to create a solid life that lends its strength to those around me.

Intertwined Faith

Though one may be overpowered,
two can defend themselves.
A cord of three strands is not quickly broken.

Ecclesiastes 4:12

I want a strong marriage. I want a connection with my husband that pulls us through the hard times and showers us with joy in the good. When I was single, I carried the burden of life's struggles on my own shoulders. But I learned to share the weight with You by asking for Your way and Your truth. Now I realize I have rested the burden of this life on the shoulders of myself and my husband...thinking this is what couples do.

I am asking You to be present in my marriage. I want us to depend on You for our every need. Let us intertwine our daily lives with our belief in You so You are always there...always at the core of who we are and what we become.

Sharing the Burden

Come to me, all you who are weary
and burdened, and I will give you rest.
Take my yoke upon you and learn from me,
for I am gentle and humble in heart,
and you will find rest for your souls.

MATTHEW 11:28-29

I have forgotten how to take up Your yoke and follow in the way You go. I am really good at picking up dirty socks, trivial information, and silly phrases...but I have forgotten how to step beside You and share what is on my plate for the day.

My eyes grow tired from staring at my list of things to do. I wish for the energy of my youth. And when I am finally too tired to keep pretending I know how to make life work, I come to You and ask for the ease of Your love and the lightness of a supported, refreshed way of living.

Gifts of the Trial

Let perseverance finish its work so that you may be mature and complete, not lacking anything.

James 1:4

I was crying over the hardship that my family is facing, and in that moment I felt so alone. I looked to You and complained that You had left us in this situation without support, without help. I didn't really believe You had abandoned me, but the ache of strife was making me doubt everything. God, You held me right then. I didn't receive the grand vision for the solution to our troubles that I had been praying for up until that point, but I received something else from You—wisdom. You revealed to me a truth that I know from my life experience but had forgotten. It is in these trials and in the act of perseverance that You *do* help us by shaping us into mature believers. Whole children of God. This trial won't break my family apart if we look to You as we press on. This trial will help us become complete in You.

FUTURE

Up Ahead

There is surely a future hope for you,
and your hope will not be cut off.

PROVERBS 23:18

I can only see what is in front of me. Yet I spend my today worrying about what I cannot know or see up ahead. Where will You take this life of mine? Where is this marriage headed? Will there be security? Joy? Have I done things that have undermined my future?

God, release my today from my tomorrow. Help me rest in the future hope You have for me. I need to let go of how I might have hurt my days ahead. I trust that You are molding, shaping, and creating a good life out of who I am and what I have done and continue to do.

A Certain Future

Do not boast about tomorrow, for you do not know what a day may bring.

PROVERBS 27:1

A leads to B leads to C, and so forth. Wouldn't it be nice if I could just follow a trail of absolutes so that I could plan on tomorrow's success? I have tried this way, but it often caused me to distance myself from Your presence. I got so caught up in doing everything right that I forgot to turn to the One who carves the right way.

I don't know what tomorrow brings. I can make wise decisions and seek Your guidance, but I need to be freed from my assumptions about what the future holds. I would rather rest in Your hands and watch as my life unfolds.

Make What You Will

Your beginnings will seem humble,
so prosperous will your future be.

Job 8:7

Here I am with all my flaws and faults. To my eyes there is not much to work with here in my life. But I want You to make what You will out of it. My hope is in You. I long to see Your hope play out in my life and my marriage. Fill my husband with the gift of possibility and joy. Breathe trust and faith into my soul.

It isn't much...this offering of my life. But I know that in Your care and with Your healing touch, it can be mighty, beautiful, and a very good life.

All of My Days

You guide me with your counsel,
and afterward you will take me into glory.

Psalm 73:24

Lord, You accompany me through my days. Your patient counsel is spoken into my heart when I remember to ask for it...and sometimes when I haven't thought to ask. My human mind and discernment lack control, focus, and understanding. But Your counsel is clear and wise. I need not depend on my questionable, easily swayed emotions because You are right here with me. Lord, I pray for a spirit that seeks Your leading right now and in every day to follow.

You want to take me by the hand through this life and into the next. Don't let me turn from You in pursuit of false dreams or because fear has told me that Your way is surely an impossible one. Help me to be wise and humble as I ask for Your counsel all of my days.

Agreement

Time for Understanding

My dear brothers and sisters, take note of this:
Everyone should be quick to listen,
slow to speak and slow to become angry.

James 1:19

Lord, help me take time before responding to my husband. Give me an adult version of a time-out to calm my perspective when I disagree with him. I find that when I give myself some space, just a touch of distance, I can see more clearly what he is trying to communicate, and then we can work toward agreement.

We will have times when we don't see eye-to-eye, but what we have going for us is a belief in You. We can turn our eyes to You for guidance when we are unsure which way to go or what to believe. Remind me, in the heat of the moment, to wait for understanding so that I speak in Your truth and not just in my haste.

Something to Believe In

For there are three that testify: the Spirit, the water and the blood; and the three are in agreement. We accept human testimony, but God's testimony is greater because it is the testimony of God, which he has given about his Son.

1 JOHN 5:7-9

There are so many different views about You. I must say, sometimes I think there is no way to know the truth. Lord, help me turn to Your Spirit for discernment and clarification when I am struggling to understand faith. When You left, You gave us the gift of the Holy Spirit so that we would have a living testimony of faith.

I want to be in agreement with people...but I am beginning to understand that this is not always possible. Direct me to agree with the Spirit so that I can rest when I disagree with humans now and then.

Two

For where two or three gather in my name, there am I with them.

Matthew 18:20

When my husband and I pray together and bring our petitions and desires before You, You promise to hear. Unlike the world we live in, You do not require a media campaign, ad blitzes, or a majority to make a thought, a need, a request valid. You hear all of our prayers…the silly little ones and the significant pleas of desperation.

Thank You for being there for us. When we do bow down, with like mind and spirit, and lift our voices… You are here, right beside us.

The Unity of Forgiveness

Forgive as the Lord forgave you.
And over all these virtues put on love,
which binds them all together in perfect unity.

Colossians 3:13-14

I have a confession, God. I have been harboring feelings of frustration and anger toward another person. It all started with a simple difference in opinion, and then it escalated. I think my pride...or maybe even my lack of confidence...turned this snowball into an avalanche. Give me a deeper, truer understanding of this conflict.

I pray for a heart that is tender toward this person. Forgiving. And desiring a positive resolution. The umbrella of Your love covers such breaks in a relationship. I see now that in disagreement...through Your perfect grace...agreement comes in the form of unity and compassion.

Compassion

You Care

Save me, O God, by your name;
vindicate me by your might.
Hear my prayer, O God; listen to
the words of my mouth.

Psalm 54:1-2

When it seems that nobody around me understands my heartache, You do. I call to You at night. I cry while I'm driving the car for errands. I lift my anxious pleas as I start my day. You hear me. You understand the words that rest in my heart that I am unable to form with my mouth.

I know that when I feel alone, You are here to comfort me. Lift me out of this time of despair, Lord. Help me see the many blessings in my life that come from Your hand. Let my woe turn to praise.

Reprieve

But now, for a brief moment, the LORD our God has been gracious in leaving us a remnant and giving us a firm place in his sanctuary, and so our God gives light to our eyes and a little relief in our bondage.

EZRA 9:8

The days that seem longest are those spent worrying about what might happen. Why is my heart today tied to the possible pitfalls of tomorrow? This bondage restricts my joy and my understanding of Your mercy and grace. Cast away my fear so that I might take refuge in Your arms of comfort.

Please give me a new life filled with moments that declare Your goodness. Turn me away from the fretful musings that occupy my mind and life today. Help me see the beauty of right now by restoring the light of Your love to my eyes.

Wandering Away

Return to the L*ORD* *your God, for he is gracious and compassionate, slow to anger and abounding in love, and he relents from sending calamity.*

JOEL 2:13

I was just going along with life when I started taking wrong turns and entertaining detours. Soon I could not find my way back to You. I knew in my heart, as I would grumble and curse the sky, that this distance was my doing and not Yours. With a humble heart I return to You and pray for Your compassion and mercy.

You are a God of justice, but also a God of gracious, limitless love. This is what I see today as I come to Your presence and ask to stay.

Harmony in the Home

Finally, all of you, be like-minded, be sympathetic, love one another, be compassionate and humble.

1 Peter 3:8

I think I finally got it today. The ideas of harmony and peace in the home became reality. I didn't have to bring in a mediator. I didn't leave. I didn't even prove that I was right. I just loved my husband and my family. I prayed for Your heart for them, and I let my ego take a vacation.

So this is what it feels like to have compassion for my family. I always thought it would come naturally because I love these people. I would do anything for them. But when You asked me to offer sympathy and to step outside of my own agenda, I faltered. Today I am back and ready to give peace a place in this home. Humble me, Lord. And lift up this family.

Forever

Longing for Home

I have seen the burden God has laid on the human race. He has made everything beautiful in its time. He has also set eternity in the human heart; yet no one can fathom what God has done from beginning to end.

ECCLESIASTES 3:10-11

It is off in the distance…the place we long for. Heaven. To me it is a confusing concept…until I think of spending forever with You, my creator. Then those ideas of beauty, perfection, and peace seem a reality.

You placed an image, an inkling of heaven in my heart. It drives me closer to Your heart. It also reminds me that the passing of time and the passing of my personal days is not a fact to be lamented. This continuation of life brings me closer to a very wonderful forever after.

Always

You have searched me, Lord, and you know me. You know when I sit and when I rise; you perceive my thoughts from afar.

Psalm 139:1-2

When I feel misunderstood by my husband or by my family and friends, I return my thoughts to the one who knows me completely—You. You in Your wisdom and might and vision created me. Before the world welcomed me with pink blankets and pacifiers, You knew everything about me. You knew the thoughts I would have. You knew the trials that would cause me to grow and learn. You saw the vista of my life from beginning to end.

Lord, thank You for always knowing me and loving me. These times of feeling misunderstood are a gift, for they lead me back to the only one who shaped my heart with His hand.

Test of Time

Give thanks to the L*ORD*, *for his love endures forever.*

2 CHRONICLES 20:21

I have purged my closet umpteen times. I have personally used up hundreds of pens and pencils. The spot where I place my book and cup of coffee on the armchair is looking worn. And my heart, which has experienced many breaks and hurts, seems to beat with wisdom and weariness. I see how all that is around me and all that *is* me feels the burden of time and use. They start to break down because they are not made for forever.

But, Lord, I have one forever in my life. One durable goodness that will persist and exist as my days wear on and all that I know and see changes. Your love will stand the test of time. And this love that is my testimony will live on after I am gone. Thank You for including me in Your gift to humanity. I love that I know Your eternal heart.

Watch for the Wind

We have this hope as an anchor for the soul, firm and secure.

HEBREWS 6:19

What is a woman supposed to hold on to in this life? Those things that I used to cling to seem unsteady and certainly unable to keep me bound to the ground when life's winds rise up. Now that marriage is a reality, I do not have a lofty view of it. I know it is work. It is a daily commitment. It is something that continues to refine me by fire.

But it is also a gift from You because it shows me how love does change and grow and hold us to Your heart. I am not naïve enough to think trouble cannot come to my home, but I do know this...my hope is in this earthly love because it is anchored in Your eternal love. It is firm and secure because it rests on ground that withstands even the mightiest storm.

GIVE AND TAKE

What Faith Takes

Just then a woman who had been subject to bleeding for twelve years came up behind him and touched the edge of his cloak. She said to herself, "If I only touch his cloak, I will be healed." Jesus turned and saw her. "Take heart, daughter," he said, "your faith has healed you." And the woman was healed from that moment.

MATTHEW 9:20-22

When I reach out to touch Your cloak...do I really believe? Am I certain like the woman You called daughter? Or am I grasping in the dark for whatever is there? Lord, give me the kind of faith that offers itself as proof of my love and belief. Give me the kind of faith that shows You I am Your daughter.

I want to reach out to You with the understanding that You will indeed feel my touch and heal my brokenness. I have been looking for ways to hold together my broken pieces for so long that I forgot to give them to You. Take this offering...it is given in faith.

The Circle of Thanks

Now, our God, we give you thanks,
and praise your glorious name.

1 Chronicles 29:13

My prayers are often loaded with a shopping list of needs and wants. They come from my very temporal view of what my life lacks. My perspective is so shallow. I realize this now that I look back on past wants. But here I am again...with a list of things I think I need. But, Lord, I realize that what I need is actually to give thanks to You for all You have given to me...for all that You are.

I stop the flow of relationship when my dialogue with You is one way. I pray like a young child who only understands how to ask for things but does not grasp gratitude. Today I offer up praise to Your holy name. I want nothing but to know You better.

The Gift of Tradition

Obey these instructions as a lasting ordinance for you and your descendants.
When you enter the land that the LORD will give you as he promised, observe this ceremony.

EXODUS 12:24-25

As my family receives abundance from Your hand, do I train them up in the ways of ceremony and tradition? Give me understanding and opportunity to show them how to give back to You, our provider. You save us from a life of meaningless pursuit. Yet we give very little of our day back to You.

Instill in me the sense of reverence You call us to have so I can share it with my family. As we enter into the promises You bestow upon us, may we always direct our prayers and actions back to You. Help us observe the acts of gratitude so that our lives become holy sacrifices to You.

Action in the Waiting

Yet the Lord *longs to be gracious to you; therefore he will rise up to show you compassion. For the* Lord *is a God of justice. Blessed are all who wait for him!*

Isaiah 30:18

Wait patiently on the Lord. Yes…I know. I have heard it before. And I wait. In the dark. In my agitated stillness I wait…wait…wait.

Wait. I sense my spirit stirring. A deeper understanding is forming in the core of myself. The waiting that seemed like punishment now shifts toward blessing. The truth of this time of stillness has not changed, but my heart has. You have moved within me to show me Your compassion.

Forgive me, Lord, for the many times I was not willing to give You my time. When I raced through the waiting, claiming I had the answer I needed or assuming You had not heard my cries…I was shortchanging the exchange You planned. Blessed is the woman who waits on Your voice. I am blessed.

LISTENING

Am I a Good Listener?

Therefore consider carefully how you listen.

Luke 8:18

Am I hearing what You are saying, Lord? When I start throwing questions at You, I can get caught up in my need and forget to really listen for Your answer. I want to be a listener who hears not only the message—the point—but also the heart behind the response.

God, teach me to be a better listener in my life. I want to be receptive to the words You are giving me to guide and shape my life. When I start spilling my thoughts to fill the void, quiet my spirit and open my ears.

Still Me

Guard your steps when you go to the house of God. Go near to listen rather than to offer the sacrifice of fools, who do not know that they do wrong. Do not be quick with your mouth, do not be hasty in your heart to utter anything before God. God is in heaven and you are on earth, so let your words be few.

Ecclesiastes 5:1-2

I trip all over my feet on my way to Your presence. I become a court jester when I want to be considered wise and worthy. What happens to me when I am in the presence of greatness? I want to be a discerning listener when I seek Your answers, Your way. Let my words be few so I can hear what You offer in the silence. Still my mumbling, my anxiousness, and my trivial ramblings.

Give me a discerning heart. Make my mind and spirit open to Your wisdom. Let me know I am a vessel waiting to be filled, and then fill me.

Add To Me

Let the wise listen and add to their learning,
and let the discerning get guidance.

PROVERBS 1:5

Lead me to a place of longing. I want to hunger for knowledge and wisdom. Sometimes I want the fast answer, but really…to make this life strong and healthy, I need deeper truths. Help me recognize the people around me who can offer godly words and guidance. I need women in my life who help me navigate life as a wife and as a woman.

I pray for a discerning spirit so I can glean from the journeys of others. When I pretend to know everything, I miss the chance to be added to, to be refined.

The Un-Dialogue

To answer before listening—that is folly and shame.

PROVERBS 18:13

Lately I have been creating a dynamic in my marriage that is useless. I ask my husband his thoughts or his opinion on something, but I already have my mind made up about what is right. And when he doesn't respond in a way that suits my idea of right and true, his opinion is not really heard by me.

God, break through my desire to be right or to have control of my shared life with my husband. I can never learn about him or from him if I continue to measure his responses and rate them against my limited perspective. Help me be an open listener so that I encounter true dialogue in my life.

SANCTUARY

Little Deaths

But my eyes are fixed on you, Sovereign LORD;*
in you I take refuge—do not give me over to death.

PSALM 141:8

Without meaning to, I give myself over to death in small ways each day. When I prefer to believe lies rather than truth. When I refuse to accept blessings and make the most of them. When I give myself over to people's false views of me rather than to the truth I know deep within. These are little deaths that destroy the peace You give to me.

Take me into Your refuge. I need a place of stillness and truthful words. I want to give myself over to life and living. Help me see ways I can restore life to my marriage and to who I am outside of my home.

The Fortress of Love

He is my loving God and my fortress, my stronghold and my deliverer, my shield, in whom I take refuge, who subdues peoples under me.

Psalm 144:2

The showers of trials and struggles fall just when I need the sun to shine. I don't feel strong enough to withstand the trouble. I need to rush to the shelter of Your love. It protects me even against the storms.

Once I enter Your fortress, I feel the calm of peace and security. It is a sanctuary where I can be myself and discover more about my life and my creator. You deliver me from harm's way and reveal to me the mysteries of grace.

What If...

Keep me safe, O God, for in you I take refuge.

Psalm 16:1

What if things don't turn out as my husband and I plan? What if our plenty turns to want and need? I worry about our life together...are we strong enough to face the difficulties that will come? Keep us safe, Lord. Guide me through the waters and bring me to a shore where I can catch my breath.

I know that Your version of safety might not come with all of the trappings of security that I pray for. My version is very comfortable and carefree. But may I have the faith and the understanding of how You work to seek Your sanctuary and to accept the safety of heart and spirit You offer.

Power in Your House

Splendor and majesty are before him;
strength and glory are in his sanctuary.

Psalm 96:6

Church is a part of my life. I find great comfort among the walls that have become familiar to me and my family. Lately though, I am realizing I need a sense of sanctuary in my life beyond church. My longing to curl up in a big chair and read Your Word is my heart's way to get back to You and Your shelter.

I need restoration throughout the week...throughout the day. May I enter Your presence with humility and come asking You for the strength I need. Let me also praise Your holy name while I take in Your beauty and comfort.

GIFTS

Gifts That Serve

*Since you are eager for gifts of the Spirit,
try to excel in those that build up the church.*

1 Corinthians 14:12

God, help me discern my spiritual gifts. I want to really tap into all the strength You have instilled in me. I want to develop these gifts and use them to serve You. When I do recognize a gift, guide me to nurture it and grow it. Allow me to see ways to build up the body of Christ through serving.

Lead me to follow the way of knowledge and understanding. Insight into my gifts will allow me to live a life of greater purpose and focus.

From Your Hand

There are different kinds of gifts, but the same Spirit distributes them. There are different kinds of service, but the same Lord. There are different kinds of working, but the same God at work. Now to each one the manifestation of the Spirit is given for the common good.

1 Corinthians 12:4-7

When I observe the gifts You have placed in my husband, I am reminded how different we are. We have different strengths and weaknesses. Sometimes we complement each other, but sometimes our differences create tension. Give me the strength to honor the gifts that are in my spouse. Help me to see You through his abilities and talents. I pray to see how You are working in his life, my life, and our shared love. Each glimpse I have into his spirit draws me closer to You and Your goodness. May we both recognize and support the gifts of the other.

What Fills the Void?

Peter replied, "Repent and be baptized, every one of you, in the name of Jesus Christ for the forgiveness of your sins. And you will receive the gift of the Holy Spirit."

Acts 2:38

The abundance of the Holy Spirit fills me with joy! When I seek Your forgiveness and repent of my sin, I feel clean and pure. This is the gift of Your Spirit and Your grace. Turn this gratitude I understand into kindness toward others.

When the blemish of my sin is removed, the void is filled with Your power and grace. This is what empowers me to move toward goodness and compassion. May I infuse my marriage with this joy that I feel. May I see each day as a gift to pass along the gifts of the Holy Spirit.

The Goodness Keeps Coming

You anoint my head with oil; my cup overflows. Surely goodness and love will follow me all the days of my life, and I will dwell in the house of the LORD forever.

PSALM 23:5-6

Thank You, God, for Your mercy and goodness. You cover me. You fill me. And Your goodness and love follow me all of my days. On the days when clouds seem to cover the blue sky, give me eyes to see the overflowing blessings in my life. I pray to never have a heart that is hardened and unable to feel deep gratitude for all that You are and all that You do for me and my family.

What can we do for You, Lord? Let this be a sincere question that rises to my mind frequently. And may I be bold enough to follow Your instructions. My husband and I live in Your house, Lord. And here we plan to remain through eternity. What can we do to serve the house of the Lord with our gift of willing hearts?

FORGIVENESS

When All Is Said and Done

Now instead, you ought to forgive and comfort him, so that he will not be overwhelmed by excessive sorrow.

2 Corinthians 2:7

Oh, God…grant me a forgiving spirit toward my husband. When he makes a mistake, I am slow to give him a break. The consequences of our mistakes are enough…our desires for repentance and forgiveness are enough.

You do not call me to be his judge or the deliverer of his punishment. You call me to comfort him when things do not go right. You lead me to extend grace so that his spirit is not consumed by regret and sorrow. They say we hurt the ones closest to us. Let me be aware of when I am too eager to hurt and reluctant to heal.

Infinity

Then Peter came to Jesus and asked,
"Lord, how many times shall I forgive my brother
or sister who sins against me? Up to seven times?"
Jesus answered, "I tell you, not seven
times, but seventy-seven times."

MATTHEW 18:21-22

When it comes to my transgressions, I seem to think I am eligible for endless forgiveness from my husband. I can be selfish, prideful, lazy, judgmental, and so many other unpleasant things. Yet I expect him to forgive me time and time again. But, Lord, I can get very stingy with my forgiveness. I start counting his sins as though I have only a few times of forgiveness in me.

What I forget is that I have Your unending forgiveness in me. It covers my life and transgressions...and it provides me with the strength and love I need to stop counting and just give freely. Forever.

Faithfully Forgiven

All the ways of the LORD are loving and faithful toward those who keep the demands of his covenant. For the sake of your name, O LORD, forgive my iniquity, though it is great.

PSALM 25:10-11

I trust Your way of love and faithfulness. My steps can be shaky along this path, but I gladly give the control over to You. Okay…I resist it a little. But I want to gladly give my life over to You. As a faithful follower, I can come to You and seek Your forgiveness.

My desire is to be true to You. My relationship with You teaches me to be a better wife and woman and human. My sins are many, but Your grace is plentiful and abundant. I pray to give this journey with You my committed effort and my love.

Wealthy

In him we have redemption through his blood, the forgiveness of sins, in accordance with the riches of God's grace.

Ephesians 1:7

I may struggle to pay all the bills each month, but I cling to my inheritance. I am Your child, and because of this I am in line to receive the riches of Your grace. You do not hold on to this wealth with a tight fist and say, "Someday." You say, "Today it is yours to have."

May I allow myself to reach for this offering. You shed Your blood so that I can stand here today and ask for forgiveness and life. I am a wealthy woman.

Honor

Strength Training

Do you not know that your bodies are temples of the Holy Spirit, who is in you, whom you have received from God? You are not your own; you were bought at a price. Therefore honor God with your bodies.

1 Corinthians 6:19-20

As I get older, I'm starting to understand how important it is to care for this body of mine. Actually… it is this body of Yours. I have borrowed it so that I can live out my life and have the joy of health and motion and strength. Lord, show me how to care for this flesh and blood so that it serves You and the purpose You have for me.

There are many voices in society claiming remedies, cures, and miracles. But I turn to You and ask for Your help as I make choices toward health and fitness. I want to honor You with my body and my life. Help me see the way to true strength and endurance. Give me the will to stay true to this effort.

You Should Be First

Honor the Lord *with your wealth, with the firstfruits of all your crops; then your barns will be filled to overflowing, and your vats will brim over with new wine.*

Proverbs 3:9-10

I pray to serve You first. My thoughts of You often come after I have given time to thoughts about my husband, my friends, myself. I forget to give You a love offering of my time and self and blessings. You don't need things. You function just fine without my praise and firstfruits...but I don't function well when I don't make offerings to You.

Release my hold on the things of this world. Let all that comes to me and my family flow through us as we first offer to You and then to others in Your name.

A New Thinking

Be devoted to one another in love.
Honor one another above yourselves.

Romans 12:10

I spent an afternoon with people recently, and I found my thoughts all related to how I was feeling or how I thought they perceived me. Halfway through the time, I felt convicted. I knew I needed to change my thinking to suit Your view of the situation. I noticed the worries and concerns of the others. Suddenly I knew how to serve each person there...but it involved letting go of my own objectives.

When I made that shift in my thinking, everything changed. I believe You used that simple encounter with others to move Your purposes forward. When I choose to honor Your children, the real work happens.

Sweet Talk

It is not good to eat too much honey,
nor is it honorable to search out
matters that are too deep.

PROVERBS 25:27

Okay, I ate it up. I couldn't help it. Someone was singing my praises, and it felt good. Thankfully I realized that I was going beyond receiving a compliment and entering that zone of ego. Because I was starving for kindness and encouragement, I forgot how to take it in.

I know that encouragement is good. Through my husband and others, You provide me with emotional support. But when I start seeking praise during times when it is about someone else or about You and not at all about me...well, then I have pursued too big of a dosage of sweetness. Help me honor You by being gracious in the presence of kind words and by directing the praise back to You.

Communication

Language of Love

I also could speak like you, if you were in my place; I could make fine speeches against you and shake my head at you. But my mouth would encourage you; comfort from my lips would bring you relief.

Job 16:4-5

The urge to repay unkindness with the same is strong in me. My husband said some hurtful words during a time when we were both not in a good frame of mind. He didn't mean to hurt me with his comments, but he did. Even after he has apologized, there is a part of me that wants to repeat hurtful words.

God, help me be a person who speaks the language of comfort and peace, even when I have been hurt. I can turn to You in prayer and read Your Word and find the solace I need. There is no reason for me to build up myself by tearing down another. Give me a lesson in Your native tongue.

Learning to Talk

They have mouths, but cannot speak,
eyes, but cannot see.
They have ears, but cannot hear, nor
is there breath in their mouths.

Psalm 135:16-17

I have a friend going through a difficult time. I am not always sure what to say in such situations. I long to be someone who offers the right words of comfort and guidance when it is my turn to speak. Keep me from becoming mute and deaf as someone in need shares her heart.

Becoming vulnerable and open will allow me to hear the words You would have me speak. Guide my thoughts and tongue to breathe living words into a situation where hope is at risk. Help me be sincere and receptive to Your leading so that I can minister.

Words for the Wordless

*Speak up for those who cannot speak for themselves,
for the rights of all who are destitute.
Speak up and judge fairly; defend
the rights of the poor and needy.*

PROVERBS 31:8-9

I want to make a difference. I try to give to charity and those in need. I pray for people who need You and Your love. Sometimes I give when it is inconvenient to do so. But when You ask me to speak for those who are unable to, I am uncomfortable...maybe because I think my identity will be shaped by the words I speak. I worry what others will think. I second-guess my motives and influence.

But it is easy and wrong to hide behind such excuses. You call me to speak out for justice. You ask me to shed light on situations where others are kept silent. Grant me the courage to speak up, Lord. Give me the strength to offer up words for the wordless.

Good Communicator

Listen to my prayer, O God, do not ignore my plea; hear me and answer me.

PSALM 55:1-2

How many times have I prayed for my husband to become a better communicator? Countless times, I'm sure. I realize it is unrealistic to have him be my soul's confidant at all times. We do have good talks. We understand each other. So I understand that the intimacy I am really seeking is that which You offer.

You do hear the heart rants and exclamations that come from me. Not only do You hear me, but You respond. Sometimes You even respond through my husband. Listen to my prayer, God. I seek Your ear and Your presence.

Love

Daily Planner

Do not those who plot evil go astray?
But those who plan what is good
find love and faithfulness.

Proverbs 14:22

Instead of troubleshooting as soon as I wake up. Instead of calling out orders or requests or inquiries to my family before everyone heads out the door… I would like to plan for goodness. What great things might happen today? What opportunities will You give me to help someone, encourage another, or enrich my life?

When I start out negative, I miss the chance to shout out for joy as the day begins. I don't want to miss the path to love and faithfulness anymore. Let my plans and projections for the day be filled with goodness.

A Fine Line

You have heard that it was said,
"Love your neighbor and hate your enemy."
But I tell you, love your enemies and
pray for those who persecute you.

MATTHEW 5:43-44

I am all for loving my neighbor, God. I really am. But what happens when my neighbor, or coworker, or peer steps over the thin line between acquaintance and nuisance? I can only avoid this person for so long. Eventually I have to be in her presence and hold my tongue.

When I give myself over to my whims of bitterness or frustration, I'm not serving You at all. I lose footing in my spiritual journey when I resort to childish behavior. Help me be a person who forgets trivial grievances and who desires reconciliation. I pray for this person and ask You to help me cross the line from old situation into the place of new, positive relationship.

Love for Everyone

Jesus replied: "'Love the Lord your God with all your heart and with all your soul and with all your mind.' This is the first and greatest commandment. And the second is like it: 'Love your neighbor as yourself.'"

Matthew 22:37-39

When my husband and I are getting along, I have a deeper love for everyone. I am kinder, gentler, more appreciative when I feel appreciated. If I investigate this further, I can see that it is when I am in Your presence and in Your Word that my heart for others changes. My capacity for love is greater.

Knowing You has given me the license to love everyone. While this can seem like a burden on some moody days, it is nonetheless freeing. The world wants to present many reasons for me to fear others, even to hate them. Your grace and love give me the excuse to love. You motivate me to give my heart without any strings attached.

The Mysteries of Love

If I have the gift of prophecy and can fathom all mysteries and all knowledge, and if I have a faith that can move mountains, but have not love, I am nothing.

1 Corinthians 13:2

The chasm between mystery and knowing is vast and powerful. It is carved out by Your hands over time and presents a challenge to anyone who seeks to believe. I peer across the void and wonder if I will ever understand the mysteries of life. When I am most bothered by this question, I realize that it is okay…no, it is a gift…to be certain of only one thing…that You love me.

Your love gives me meaning. Your love allows me to love. And as I see my life with my husband unfolding and growing, I do believe that it is the knowledge of Your love that moves me toward purpose and identity.

Belief

Start with Belief

But we ought always to thank God for you,
brothers and sisters loved by the Lord,
because God chose you as firstfruits to be saved
through the sanctifying work of the Spirit
and through belief in the truth.

2 Thessalonians 2:13

Going back to the beginning is not easy for me. I think I have come so far in my spiritual quest...but I still need to return to my need to believe in truth. This desire leads me forward when life brings questions that perplex me rather than calm me. You chose me to be saved through Your Spirit and through truth. Truth beckoned me to Your heart and keeps me in Your presence.

Return me to that preference for truth. Lead me away from falseness and deceit that looks appealing. Restore in me the truth of salvation so that I never sell it for the world's false peace.

Taking Up the Offer

Then he said to Thomas,
"Put your finger here; see my hands.
Reach out your hand and put it into my
side. Stop doubting and believe."

John 20:27

You must get so tired of me doubting, Lord. I am a curious and hard-to-convince woman…just ask my husband. He has to deal with my doubt in our daily life. All the questions. This must get tiring. Yet You never stop meeting me at least halfway to present me with an obvious truth. It jolts me back into the reality of Your love.

I'm sorry that I am one of those people who asks to see Your hands again and again. But thank You for extending them to me, along with the offer to feel, believe, and stop doubting. You save me every time.

For Once

If you declare with your mouth, "Jesus is Lord," and believe in your heart that God raised him from the dead, you will be saved.

ROMANS 10:9

My inability to be quiet used to seem like a curse. But my desire to share myself and my opinion with others seems to serve my faith well. I don't have to hold back my love for You and my belief in who You are. I can say "Jesus is Lord" without wondering if I should have kept my mouth shut.

Every time I see the joy of someone discovering Your identity and role in her life, I am given another reason to shout out with happiness. It does my heart good to join the voices of others when praising Your holy name. For once, my open expression of my opinion serves a good purpose.

At the Feet of the Master

The woman came and knelt before him.
"Lord, help me!" she said.
He replied, "It is not right to take the children's bread and toss it to their dogs."
"Yes it is, Lord," she said. "Even the dogs eat the crumbs that fall from their masters' table."
Then Jesus said to her, "Woman, you have great faith! Your request is granted."
And her daughter was healed at that moment.

Matthew 15:25-28

If You were sitting here at my table, would I speak to You of what I need with boldness? Or would I cower and apologize and present my petition with a defeated faith? I have so much respect for people who turn to You at all times and ask for Your presence and power. Give me that kind of faith, Lord.

Would You hear my voice if I were to speak from my current level of faith? Would I state my case for wanting to live in Your will and from Your hand of provision? I pray that I become a person who never cries wolf…but cries out to You with sincerity and great faith.

FAITHFULNESS

My Worth

A wife of noble character who can find?
She is worth far more than rubies.

PROVERBS 31:10

Because of my identity in You, I have learned that my value comes from You alone and not from others, from my job, from my status, from my clothes. But lately You have been showing me how I can have value through my character. My life has more meaning and significance when I honor my marriage and this life You have given me.

Life is not always easy, but when hard times hit or good times surface, the care I pour into my marriage does reflect the condition of my heart. Help me be an honorable, faithful, and loving wife. Show me how I can achieve beauty that is soul deep when I give my heart gladly to my true love.

Slippery Slope

Her husband has full confidence
in her and lacks nothing of value.
She brings him good, not harm,
all the days of her life.

Proverbs 31:11-12

I would never bring harm to my husband. I would never make him a low priority in my life…Uh-oh. I think I spoke too soon. Looking back a few years ago, I gave myself over to work and success. It was for all the right reasons at the time. But now I'm not so sure.

God, reveal to me the ways in which I am unfaithful to my marriage. May I always see false motives before they take control of my thoughts and behaviors. I don't want to put my husband second to anything but You. To put monetary goals above matrimony purposes would be a disservice to You and to this shared life.

Up to the Task

She considers a field and buys it; out of her earnings she plants a vineyard. She sets about her work vigorously; her arms are strong for her tasks.

Proverbs 31:16-17

The work of marriage is giving me mighty muscles. When I was young, love was easy. I loved my parents, my friends, and had occasional crushes on boys at school. But now, as a woman, I see that love requires work and perseverance. I have discovered that being a wife demands sweat equity. Giving up is not an option if this love is to grow strong and resilient. Help me to be faithful in all things.

Lord, today I pray for Your patience and Your love. Give me arms, legs, and a heart that can handle the effort involved in this life. Help me build a relationship that is a testament to this work. Thank You for showing me that there is joy and satisfaction when marriage becomes a labor of love.

The Good Life

She is clothed with strength and dignity; she can laugh at the days to come. She speaks with wisdom, and faithful instruction is on her tongue. She watches over the affairs of her household and does not eat the bread of idleness. Her children arise and call her blessed; her husband also, and he praises her: "Many women do noble things, but you surpass them all."

Proverbs 31:25-29

God, give me Your priorities for my life. I want a good life. I pray to reach the end of my days with a heart that is full of gratitude, contentment, and faith. Do not let me waste my emotions and my efforts on unimportant matters. I see how the hours of my day can be given over to fretting or complaining, and it shocks me. This is not who I want to be. You have placed me in this position of honor and blessing. May I serve my family gladly while also understanding the purpose You call me to walk in. Bring to my plate those things that are important to You so that my family will call me faithful, wise, and compassionate.

Committed to Commitment

Commit your way to the LORD;
trust in him and he will do this:
He will make your righteous
reward shine like the dawn,
your vindication like the noonday sun.

PSALM 37:5-6

Lord, bless my marriage with a deepened level of commitment. Give my husband and me hearts that can expand to take in the flaws and weaknesses of the other with grace. When we step forward together, committed to commitment, we will greet the future with the strength of two. Help me to notice when his heart needs encouragement to trust in You. Lead him to support me in my faith journey. If there's an area of weakness in our relationship, give us the tools and the desire to repair that area and tend to it with vigilance.

Humble our hearts to serve You with all that we are. Let us be a light to others in our faithfulness to one another and to You.

About the Author

Hope Lyda is an author whose devotionals, novels, and prayer books, including the popular *One-Minute Prayers® for Women* and *Life as a Prayer,* have sold over one million copies. Her inspirational books reflect her desire to embrace and deepen faith while journeying to God's mystery and wonder.

Hope has worked in publishing for more than 20 years, writing and coming alongside other writers to help them shape their heart messages. As a trained spiritual director, she loves to help others enter God's presence and pay attention to their authentic, unique life and purpose. Her greatest joy is to find ways to extend these invitations through the written word and writing exercises.

She and her husband, Marc, have been married for more than 25 years and live in Oregon.

Find out more about Hope, her books, and her heart at www.hopelyda.com

More favorite reads from Hope Lyda

Life as a Prayer

One Minute with Jesus for Women

One-Minute Prayers® for Moms

One-Minute Prayers® for Women Gift Edition

One-Minute Prayers® for Comfort and Healing

One-Minute Prayers® to Begin and End Your Day

This Little Light of Mine

Available in e-book only:

One-Minute Prayers® for Young Women

Hip to Be Square (fiction)

Altar Call (fiction)

Life, Libby, and the Pursuit of Happiness (fiction)

To learn more about Harvest House books and to read sample chapters, visit our website:

www.harvesthousepublishers.com